SOCR
IN THE AGORA

AMERICAN SCHOOL OF
CLASSICAL STUDIES AT ATHENS
PRINCETON, NEW JERSEY
1978

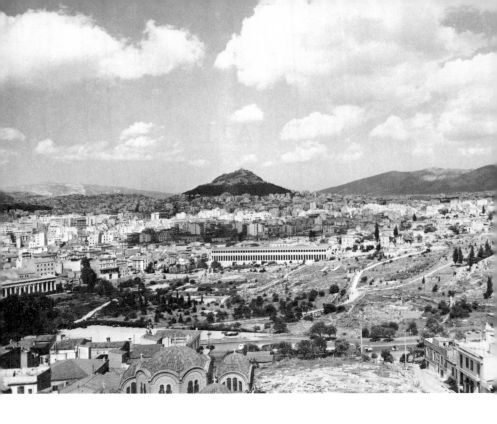

'Everything combines to make our knowledge of Socrates himself a subject of Socratic irony. The only thing we know definitely about him is that we know nothing.' —L. Brunschvicg

As far as we know Socrates himself wrote nothing, yet not only were his life and words given dramatic attention in his own time in the *Clouds* of Aristophanes, but they have also become the subject of many others' writing in the centuries since his death. Fourth-century B.C. writers who had first-hand knowledge of him composed either dialogues in which he was the dominant figure (Plato and Aeschines) or memories of his teaching and activities (Xenophon). Later authors down even to the present day have written numerous biographies based on these early sources and considering this most protean of philosophers from every possible point of view except perhaps the topographical one which is attempted here. Instead of putting Socrates in the context of 5th-century B.C. philosophy, politics, ethics or rhetoric, we shall look to find him in the material world and physical surroundings of his favorite stamping-grounds, the Athenian Agora.

Just as 'agora' in its original sense meant 'gathering place' but came in time to mean 'market place', so the agora itself was originally a gathering place

1. Agora from the west, with clouds.

Strepsiades: By Zeus, I beg you, Socrates, say who these are that sing this solemn chorus? Are they heroines of old?

Socrates: No, but Clouds of heaven, the mighty goddesses of the leisure class who give us judgment, eloquence and wit.

*   *   *

Clouds: Greetings, old sir, hot on the track of culture, and you, too, high-priest of infinite subtleties, tell us what you require. For to no other of the scientologists would we so listen except Prodicus, because he is wise, but to you because you swagger in the streets looking askance, and barefoot you endure a hard life priding yourself on our favor.

Aristophanes, *Clouds* 314 ff.

which became by use over time the market place. That a place where people gather should become the scene of buying and selling (the Greek verb is *agorazein*, to frequent the agora) is reasonable, but for the Greeks the market aspect of the agora was but a by-product of any gathering's chief function: talk (the Greek verb is *agoreuein*). Such talk might be political haranguing or common gossip, philosophical inquiry or hard bargaining, but it was the one permanent feature in the kaleidoscopic Greek scene. Therefore, it was in the Athenian Agora that Socrates, pre-eminent among Greek word-merchants, was mostly to be found. According to his younger contemporary Xenophon, 'he was always on public view; for early in the morning he used to go to the walkways and gymnasia, to appear in the agora as it filled up, and to be present wherever he would meet with the most people' (*Memorabilia* I.i.10). And as Plato makes Socrates himself say in the *Apology* (17c): 'If you hear me making my defence in the same language I customarily use both elsewhere and in the agora at the tables where many of you have heard me, do not marvel or raise a clamor on this account.'

Since the Greek word for table (*trapeza*) is still used in modern Greek for bank, Socrates' reference here must be to little stands set up by money-changers and money-lenders, who must have been as numerous as they were indispensable in a land where every city minted its own coins on a variety of standards. Although for a later period there is some evidence that the tables were more or less permanently set up in a particular quarter of the agora, in Socrates' time it is most likely that the money-changers, like the Sausage-seller in Aristophanes' *Knights*, set up shop with portable tables wherever men might be gathered together to buy and sell. Such places would be equally attractive to the philosopher intent on the exchange of ideas rather than coins or material goods. Surely Socrates' answer to Phaedrus' gentle teasing in the Platonic dialogue (230cd) makes explicit his way of life and its rationale even though he may never have put it into these words:

> *Phaedrus*: How very strange you are, sir. You talk like a tourist rather than a native. You apparently never set foot in the country or go outside the city wall.
>
> *Socrates*: Look at it my way, my good friend. It is because I love knowledge, and it is the people in the city who teach me, not the country or the trees.

Since Socrates was most truly at home in Athens' agora, it should be possible to follow his career in the remains there and rebuild in ideal form the surroundings in which he practiced what he preached: 'the unexamined life is not worth living' (*Apology* 38a).

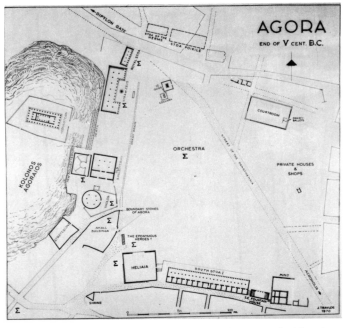

2. Plan of the Agora in the late 5th century B.C. Sigma-marked locations indicate that 'Socrates was here.'

THE AGORA is a good proving ground for attempts to reconcile conflicting bits of evidence about Socrates' attitude to the gods of his contemporaries and countrymen. Although Aristophanes portrays him as trying to wean Strepsiades from the Olympian gods and as swearing by physical principles like Air, Chaos and Respiration, Xenophon asserts (*Memorabilia* I.i.2) that Socrates 'was frequently seen sacrificing on the public altars of the city.' Later when he was indicted for impiety, part of the charge against him was that he did not believe in the gods in whom the city believed but introduced new divinities. In Socrates' own speech of defence, for which we have the presumably independent testimony of both Plato and Xenophon, he not only called upon the god of Delphi as a witness to his wisdom but justified as service to that god his unpopular practice of exposing other men's pretensions to wisdom. And as for introducing new divinities, there was only the 'voice' or 'sign' which Xenophon has him put forward as a special sign of divine favor—the way in which the known gods spoke to him as they spoke to others in omens, signs or oracles.

Socrates' sign may be thought of as evidence of the divine protection apparently promised by the oracle given to his father while he was still a child: 'Let the boy do whatever comes into his mind and do not restrain him but give him his head, not bothering about him except to pray on his behalf to

3. Restored drawing of the Altar of the Twelve Gods, the center from which distances were measured, established in 522/1 B.C., destroyed by the Persians in 480/79 B.C. and rebuilt in the latter part of Socrates' lifetime.

4. A 4th-century B.C. altar which was moved to the Agora in the 1st century, probably from the Athenian assembly place on the Pnyx. Its size and two locations suggest that it is the altar of Zeus Agoraios, known to be established both in the Agora and in the Assembly Place.

Zeus Agoraios and the Muses' (Plutarch, *de genio Socratis* 20). Even if this oracle is apocryphal, it illustrates the extent to which Socrates was associated in the popular mind with the chief god of the Agora and seemed to be almost as much a fixture of the Agora as that god.

SOCRATES' dealings with his fellow citizens, no less than with their gods, showed his peculiar genius. Where other Athenians considered political action to be the only true vocation for a free man, Socrates avoided public office for the most part and preferred to exercise his powers of persuasion on a man-to-man basis. He did, however, serve a term on the Boule, the council which prepared legislation for the Assembly and in which each year five hundred men chosen by lot not only served as members but also took a turn at presiding. Concerning Socrates' stint as president Plato has him tell how he was supposed to take the vote but did not know how and was much laughed at in consequence (*Gorgias* 474a). Whether this failure was actual or figurative is not so important as the way he uses it in the dialogue to introduce his preference, so often expressed elsewhere, for the opinion of the one man who

5. Model of New Bouleuterion, built in the last quarter of the 5th century B.C. to the west (left) of the original building which was later rebuilt as the Metroon to house the shrine of the Mother of the Gods and the public archives. The round building is the Tholos.

knows to the opinion of the many who are ignorant about the matter under discussion.

During Socrates' term in the Boule (406/5 B.C.) the great loss of ships and men after the victory at Arginusae so angered the Athenians that they were ready to condemn the generals as a group without individual due process. In the *Apology* (32b) of Plato Socrates says, 'Then I alone of those in charge opposed such illegal action.' Xenophon's account is fuller (*Memorabilia* I.i.18): 'Serving in the Boule and having sworn the bouleutic oath [that he would serve in accordance with the laws], and being in charge in the Assembly, when the People wished to put all nine generals to death by a single vote contrary to the laws, he refused to put the vote. . . . He considered it more important to keep his oath than to please the People by doing wrong. . . . For he did not believe that the gods cared for men as the many believed; for they think the gods know some things but not others; Socrates thought that the gods know all things, . . . that they are everywhere and give signs to men about all human affairs.' This report shows not only Xenophon's belief in Socrates' true piety but confirms and justifies Socrates' resolve to practice privately rather than politically, for 'Do you think that I would have survived so many years if I had acted officially and supported what was just? Far from it, gentlemen!' (Plato, *Apology* 32e).

SOCRATES' experience of public life under the Thirty Tyrants was as discouraging as that in the democracy. When Socrates and four other citizens were summoned to the Tholos by the Thirty and ordered to bring in one Leon for execution, the four went after Leon, but Socrates went quietly home, thus foiling the oligarchs' attempt to implicate him in their crimes (*Apology* 32cd): 'And perhaps I would myself have been put to death because of this if the regime had not soon been overthrown.'

Xenophon (*Memorabilia* I.ii.32) seems to be exemplifying Socrates' penchant for homely comparisons when he has him say in this context: 'I would find it marvelous if a cowherd who reduced the number and value of his flock did not admit to being a bad herdsman, and still more marvelous if the governor of a city who reduced the number and quality of its citizens was not ashamed and did not think himself a bad guardian.'

THE AGORA was not only the center of the Athenian administration and politics which Socrates so prudently for the most part eschewed but also the scene of gatherings for all kinds of exchange, ranging from gossip and philosophical discussion to the buying and selling of every imaginable requirement

6. Interior of the Tholos, sometimes called Skias or sunshade from the shape of its roof. A small kitchen on the north side made it possible for those presiding in the Bouleuterion to remain on duty and dine 'on the job.' Socrates would have eaten here when he presided in 406/5 B.C., and it was here that the Thirty Tyrants had their headquarters when they usurped the power in 403 B.C.

of the body politic. The mixture is neatly summed up by the comic poet Eubulus: 'You will find everything sold together in the same place in Athens: figs, witnesses to summonses, bunches of grapes, turnips, pears, apples, givers of evidence, roses, medlars, porridge, honey-combs, chick-peas, law-suits, beestings-puddings, myrtle, allotment-machines, irises, lambs, water-clocks, laws, indictments.' Socrates' reaction to this profusion is characteristic: 'After looking at the number of things on sale, he used to say to himself, "How many things I do not need!" and he used regularly to recite these verses: "Silver and purple are fine things for tragedians, but not for real life" ' (Diogenes Laertius ii.25).

SOCRATES' interest was much more in the trading of ideas, and this pursuit took him to places where he might find individuals or groups ready and eager for talk. Since Plato did not write history we can not know that Socrates held a particular conversation in a specific place, but surely the scenes in which the Dialogues are set had to be places where contemporary readers would have expected such discussions to take place. Plato locates some dialogues in private houses, but public buildings both outside the Agora and within also provide appropriate settings. It was in the Stoa Basileios where the Archon Basileus

7. Restored drawing of the northwest corner of the Agora: at extreme left is a corner of the Stoa of Zeus, then the Stoa Basileios (Royal Stoa); across the Panathenaic Way the as yet unexcavated Stoa of the Herms; center front, a shrine.

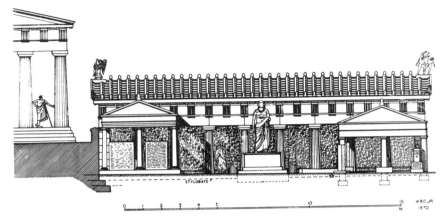

8. Drawing of Stoa Basileios. Here the laws of Solon were set up; here the archons took their oath of office; and here, presumably because it was the King Archon's office, the Court of the Areopagus met on occasion to conduct business.

held court as Athens' chief religious officer that the *Euthyphro* is set, and the discussion about piety results naturally from the two speakers' presence there: Socrates as defendant on a charge of impiety and Euthyphro as prosecutor of his father for murder. Since Euthyphro asserts that he is acting out of piety, the resulting dialogue presents the delightfully ironic picture of the 'pious' man being tested by the man charged with impiety. Although no definition is arrived at, Euthyphro finds himself retreating from one position after another as he is unable to defend it against Socratic questioning. It is this power of Socrates about which one Nicias warns Lysimachus in another dialogue (*Laches* 187d): 'You do not seem to know that whoever becomes involved in discussion with Socrates, no matter what the original topic was, can not help but be led on by him until he has given a complete account of himself; and Socrates will not let him go until he has well and truly sifted him.'

As the Stoa Basileios serves as the setting for the talk with Euthyphro, so it is also used as Socrates' destination when he concludes his effort to bring Theaetetus' idea of knowledge to birth (210d): 'Both I and my mother were endowed by the god with the midwife's art; she delivered women, but I deliver young men who are noble and fair. Now I must go to the Stoa of the Basileus to answer Meletus' charge against me. Let us meet here tomorrow morning again.' Not only does this parting shot show the contrast between Socrates' 'profession' of helping the young and Meletus' charge against him of corrupting the young, but also it reflects what may have been the crowded nature of Socrates' schedule: a conversation of more than sixty pages with

9. Model of the Stoa of Zeus Eleutherios (left of center in foreground).

Theaetetus followed by one of some fifteen pages with Euthyphro—all before his meeting with the magistrate—and on the next day the continuation which we have in the fifty-odd pages of the *Sophist*. No wonder his shrewish wife Xanthippe complained about his failure as a breadwinner! Thus it might have been when the family was suffering more than usually from lack of support that the following scene occurred: 'Once when she tore off his cloak in the Agora and his friends urged him to hit back, he said, "Yes indeed, so that while we spar you may egg us on with a 'Good hit, Socrates!' 'Well done, Xanthippe!' " ' (Diogenes Laertius ii.37).

THE STOA OF ZEUS ELEUTHERIOS, a much larger building immediately to the south of the Stoa Basileios, provides the setting for two other dialogues: *Eryxias* and *Theages*. Although both are included in the Platonic corpus, neither is thought to be genuine, but this may make the probability of their setting all the greater since imitators would take especial care to achieve verisimilitude. In the *Theages* (121a) Demodocus meets Socrates and wishing to consult him asks, 'Would you come away here out of the traffic into the Stoa of Zeus Eleutherios?' That the Stoa afforded not only shelter from the market-place bustle and the elements but also places in which to sit becomes clear from the *Eryxias* (392a): 'Eryxias and I happened to be strolling about in the

10. Boundary stone, probably of Zeus Eleutherios, and originally part of a wall marking the limit of the sanctuary: *Dios E[   ]*, i.e., 'of Zeus E[leutherios].'

Stoa of Zeus Eleutherios when Critias and Erasistratus came up. . . . "Do you wish," he said, "to sit down first? For I am tired from having walked yesterday from Megara." ' Not only pseudo-Plato but also Aeschines used the Stoa; the beginning of his dialogue *Miltiades* is preserved on a bit of papyrus (Socrates is speaking): 'During the procession of the Great Panathenaea we were sitting (Hagnon father of Theramenes, Euripides the poet and I) in the Stoa of Zeus Eleutherius, and Miltiades passed close by us.' And in Xenophon's *Oeconomicus* (vii.1) Socrates says, 'So once seeing him sitting in the Stoa of Zeus Eleutherius apparently at leisure, I went up and sat beside him, asking, "Why are you sitting here, Ischomachus?" '

SINCE Socrates was 'always spending time wherever the young men were involved in any noble study or pursuit' (*Laches* 180c), the location of some dialogues in the Lyceum and one or another palaestra is not surprising. A palaestra in particular was a place where young and old could meet on the common ground of sport and go on to more intellectual matters. So in Plato's *Lysis* (204a) when Socrates is waylaid on the road from the Academy to the Lyceum and invited to enter an open door:

'What is this place and what goes on here?'
'It is a palaestra, newly built, and there is a great deal of conversation which we would gladly share with you.'
. . . Entering we found the boys, who were all dressed up, just completing the sacrifice, for that part of the rites was almost finished, and playing games with knucklebones.

11. Red-figured vases from the Agora with palaestra scenes. The cup at left was found in one of the Prison cells.

The more usual activities in the palaestra, wrestling and gymnastics, provided Socrates with the kind of text he liked to expound: training of the body, the harmony of body and soul, and their incompatibility.

MANY of Socrates' discussions seem to have taken place, as he himself says in the *Apology* of Plato, near 'the tables' in the open parts of the Agora and, as other sources indicate, in various shops and workshops round about. Favorite gathering places for talk and exchange of gossip were the barber's, the perfume-seller's, the cobbler's and the wreath-market. That Socrates frequented these and others is clear both from the extent to which his talk is full of homely examples taken from the various crafts and from the reports of such visits in Xenophon's *Memorabilia* (III.x); among these latter were a painter, a sculptor and an armorer. Socrates questioned them about their crafts in such a way as to give them some understanding and insight into what they had previously done unthinkingly. Their chagrin at being shown how little they knew of that of which they thought themselves masters may have been compensated to some extent by the number of potential customers Socrates' talk attracted. And yet it is not clear whether he undertook such questioning because he was impressed by their skill and thought that in them he might find refutation of the god's assertion that no one was wiser than Socrates or whether he was trying to understand how it is possible to create real things in imitation of the ideal and so to grasp something of the divine prototype.

Xenophon tells also (*Memorabilia* IV.ii) of a leather-worker (rein-maker or saddler) to whose workshop very near the Agora the learned youth Euthydemus used to come, since he was too young to enter the Agora. Socrates sought him out there, wishing to question him about the wisdom to be gained from books, of which the young man had a large collection. That this leather-worker was the same as the cobbler Simon whose place of work has been identified just outside the Agora seems most probable. Simon was not only himself a student of philosophy but also the first to write Socratic dialogues, taking notes when Socrates came to his shop and conversed with other visitors. The titles of 33 so-called Cobbler's Dialogues are preserved and echo the interests shown by Socrates in the surviving Platonic dialogues (Diogenes Laertius ii.122).

Among the pleasant ancient forgeries of no philosophical importance that have come down to us as Letters of Socrates is a note addressed to Simon by Aristippus of Cyrene, a pupil of Socrates and founder of the Cyrenaic School. The letter reads in part:

> I marvel and applaud, if being but a cobbler you were wise enough to persuade Socrates and the fairest, best born youths to sit with you—such youths as Alcibiades son of Clinias, Phaedrus the Myrrhinousian, and Euthydemus son of Glaucus—and men of affairs too, like Epistrates the

12. A 4th-century B.C. cobbler's dedication depicting his shop.

Shieldbearer and Euryptolemus and the others. Indeed if Pericles were not involved in official duties and in war, he too would be with you.

It is a pleasant picture: the small sunny courtyard where the cobbler perhaps did not always stick to his last and a select company attempted to define eternal verities. Simon's shop provides an ancient parallel (hence endowed with greater dignity and significance) for the early American country store with its cracker-barrel philosophers. Or perhaps the society attracted to the blacksmith's forge the world over is more pertinent, since there is something fascinating about the deft movements and skillful performance of a master craftsman that draws onlookers who come to marvel and stay to talk. Somehow the artisan's productive energy and the very process of creation releases inhibitions and stimulates speculation on the causes of things and their rightness.

WHEN TALK was the chief entertainment after dinner as in the *Symposium* of Plato, the setting was a private house. We do not know where the house of Agathon was and may imagine that its probably anonymous remains lie somewhere under or within the cellars of modern Athens. But we do have samples of houses that belong to Socrates' time just off the Street of the Marble Workers (so-called by the excavator) which leads out of the Agora to the southwest. That Socrates was familiar with this road is probable from an anecdote reported by Plutarch (*de genio Socratis* 10): 'Socrates was walking

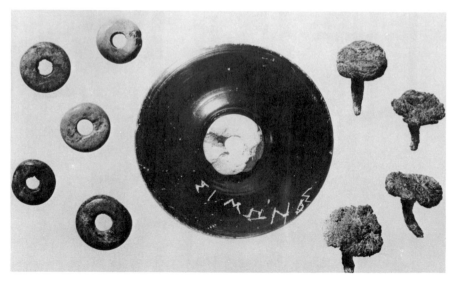

13. Foot of a black-glazed kylix on which is scratched *Simonos* (Simon's); this along with the hobnails and bone rings for laced boots clinch the identification of Simon's shop, in and near which all were found.

toward the house of Andocides, questioning and teasing Euthyphron, when suddenly he stood still, stopped talking, and fell into a kind of trance. Then, turning, he went along the street of the cabinetmakers . . . but some of the young men, wishing to test Socrates' "sign", went straight on. . . . And as they were going through the marble-workers' quarter past the lawcourts, a flock of pigs met them, all covered with filth and jostling one another; since there was no turning off, the pigs ran some of them down and covered the others with dirt.' It seems obvious that Socrates had intended to go through the marble-workers' quarter but his sign had warned him off, presumably having foreseen the flock of pigs! Although the anecdote may caricature Socrates' sign, there is no reason to doubt the setting.

Agathon's house in the *Symposium* must have been very like the larger of these 5th-century houses in the Street of the Marble Workers. The party was going on in the *andron* just off the court, which was entered by a long corridor from the house door. The men hear a great knocking at the door; an attendant is sent; and shortly they hear the voice of Alcibiades in the court. No evidence has survived here of the dining couches, but it seems likely that dining couches in private houses were movable, for the sake of more flexible ar-

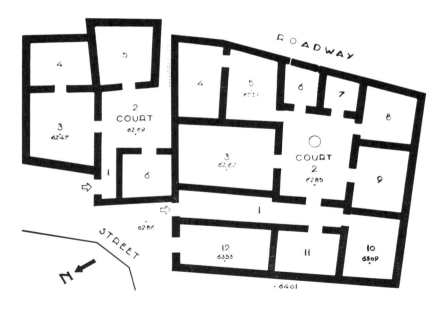

14. Plan of houses on the Street of the Marble Workers. The larger one on the right might be like Agathon's. The vestibule of the smaller house on the left would have been handy for the trance of Socrates that delayed his arrival at the party.

rangements, and so we should not expect the special floor preparation we find in public dining rooms for the presumably permanent accommodation of couches. In the *Symposium* the three-to-a-couch arrangement surely requires that the couches head inward and so presents a completely different picture from that seen in a series of official dining rooms in a 5th-century stoa along the southern border of the Agora. The more formal arrangement is what Socrates would have experienced if the jury of 500 solid Athenian citizens at his trial had seen fit to award him the penalty he proposed in answer to the death penalty proposed by his accusers: the privilege of dining at the state's expense in the Prytaneion which was ordinarily granted to benefactors of the state. And as Socrates says in the *Apology* of Plato: 'What then is fitting for a poor man who is your benefactor, one who needs leisure in order to continue exhorting you? There is nothing more fitting than for such a man to be maintained in the Prytaneion, much more than someone who wins a victory in the Olympic Games. For such a man makes you appear blessed, but I help you to be blessed; and he has no need of support, while I do' (36de).

Perhaps on the principle of *in vino veritas* the portrait of Socrates in the *Symposium* seems to be a truer and more intimate one than we have elsewhere

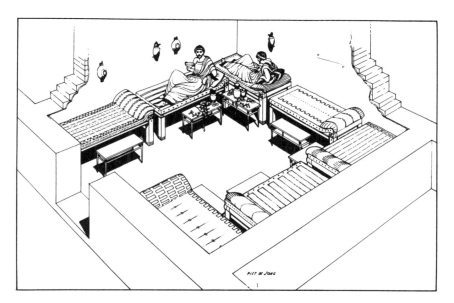

15. Arrangement of couches in a room of South Stoa I, where the off-center door allowed seven couches to be arranged on the slightly raised pebble-and-cement border around the room. (Is it a coincidence that even in the differently arranged dining room of Agathon there were seven men before Alcibiades burst in?)

in the rich Socratic literature. From the very beginning when Aristodemus on meeting him is struck by his unusual state—wearing sandals and fresh from the bath—the man's quality of mind-above-matter is clear, and his fit of abstraction on the very doorstep reminds us of his ability so to withdraw from the real world as to become almost a Platonic idea, or at least so as to feel, apparently, neither fatigue nor cold. And yet, he was intensely human, as is evident from the teasing affection in which he was held by men as disparate as the party assembled in Agathon's house: the host himself, who was celebrating a victory in the tragic contest, is more appreciative of praise from Socrates than of the plaudits of the multitude; Phaedrus, the eager young rhetorician, gently chides him for his inability to stop talking; the physician Eryximachus admires his ability to cope with both wine and love; Aristophanes, although his comedy about Socrates undoubtedly helped build the prejudice that culminated in the charge of impiety, here consorts with him on the friendliest of terms. But it is Alcibiades, nephew of Pericles and spoiled darling of the Athenian democracy, whose feelings for Socrates reveal most clearly the power of attraction he exercised on the best and the brightest and

16. Black-figured vase from the Agora with a different kind of symposium: man and woman carousing.

the strength of his influence. Amid much joking and teasing Alcibiades lovingly and disrespectfully sings his praises as one who conquers all men in speech, who charms men's souls with his talk and whose virtuous actions speak louder even than his words. This is the Alcibiades whose passionate pride, avid appetites and political ambition made him both agent and symbol of Athenian imperialistic excesses. His meteoric rise and dramatic descent, his triumphant restoration and tragic fall led Athenians who were thus twice disappointed of the high hopes he had raised to find some outlet for their frustration and someone to blame. And so ironically enough it was the very man whose influence for good shamed Alcibiades who undeservedly earned the reputation of corrupting the young. Plato seems concerned to explain here how it was Socrates' attractiveness to Alcibiades that produced such negative results (*Symposium* 216ab): 'He alone makes me feel shame. For I know that I can neither refute him nor say that I do not have to do what he urges, but I know that as soon as I go away I am overcome by the favor of the multitude. And so I run away and avoid him. . . .'

17. Two ostraca (potsherds) with the name of Alcibiades son of Cleinias. Athenian ostracism (potsherd voting) was designed to save the democracy from too great concentration of power in one man, and so the vote was to determine if someone should go into exile for ten years. Alcibiades did not 'win' in the voting for which these sherds were prepared but later fled to avoid a death penalty. This piece of roof tile was obviously broken to make two ballots, and the line of the break at the right suggests there might have been a third.

18. Terracotta bearded male head of the Silen type. This handmade piece with modeled eyeballs might represent a teacher rather than a Silen since examples of the two types are much the same. Earliest 3rd century B.C.

IT IS ALSO Alcibiades in the *Symposium* who gives us the most memorable picture of Socrates: 'I shall try to praise Socrates with a simile. Perhaps he will think it rather ridiculous, but imagery is for truth-telling, not poking fun. For I insist that he is most like those Silens in the statuaries' shops which are seen on being opened to have images of gods inside.' The divinity of the inner man is made abundantly clear in all of Plato's dialogues, but for the appearance of the outer man Xenophon's *Symposium* provides the best evidence (v.5–7); Socrates lures Critobulus into defining beauty as functionalism and then catalogues the assets by which he expects to win the beauty contest:

> Your eyes see only straight ahead, but mine see also to the side, since they project. . . .
> Your nostrils look to the ground, but mine flare so as to receive smells from all sides. . . . My flat nose does not block my vision but allows my eyes to see whatever they wish.

His competitor, Critobulus, continues: 'I yield to your mouth for if mouths are made for biting you can take a bigger bite than I can. And do you not think your kiss is softer because of your thick lips?'

THE DRAMATIC DATE of Plato's *Symposium* is just a year before another drinking party during which Alcibiades indulged along with relatives and friends not in philosophical discussion but in a parody of the sacred Mysteries —and this in the presence of non-initiates. At least so the charge of impiety

19. A fragment of an Attic stele, on some ten of which were recorded the sale of property confiscated from Alcibiades and his associates after their conviction on a charge of impiety in 415 B.C. One subtotal comprising the sale of slaves and a piece of land belonging to Alcibiades' uncle Axiochus is recorded as 672 drachmas (including the sales tax).

ran, whether it was true or trumped up by political enemies envious of Alcibiades' great popularity and influence. But it is perhaps a commentary on ordinary men's resentment of their extraordinary fellows that the same charge of impiety was brought against both the wayward pupil and his sober master, on the one hand for an evening's entertainment and for a lifetime of earnest effort on the other. Socrates was to pay with his life, but Alcibiades escaped with the loss of his property which was confiscated and sold for what must have been a remarkable sum, if we may judge from a preserved subtotal for one of his comrades, Oionias: 81 talents, 2000 drachmas (488,000 dr.).

In this connection Socrates' estimate of his own fortune is interesting (Xenophon, *Oeconomicus* ii.2-4):

> *Socrates*: And yet, Critobulus, you seem to me quite poor, and there are times I feel very sorry for you.
>
> *Critobulus*: And how much do you think your property would bring if sold, and how much would mine?

Socrates: I expect if I found a good buyer, everything including the house would bring 500 drachmas; but yours would sell for more than a hundred times as much.

Critobulus: And even so you think you are in no need of money but pity me for my poverty?

Socrates: Yes, for mine is enough to satisfy my needs, but for your style of life . . . , you would not have enough with three times as much as you have.

Socrates' view of wealth is further amusingly tied to the Agora in the pseudo-Platonic dialogue *Eryxias* (399e–400d):

Socrates: Still then it would remain to consider what money is. . . . Each of these things (leather, iron, stones) are clearly not money if their possessors are not made more wealthy thereby. . . . If we should wish to consider . . . why leather is money for the Carthaginians but not for us, or why iron is money for the Spartans but not for us, would we find some such answer as this? If someone in Athens should acquire a thousand talents' weight of these stones in the Agora, for which we have no use, would he in any way be thought the richer for this?

20. A view of the Panathenaic Way as it climbs from the Agora toward the Acropolis shows a wealth of stones such as Socrates considered the Agora could provide.

21. Drawing of the Eponymous Heroes as they were re-established in the 4th century B.C. Only traces of the 5th-century monument are now recognizable under the foundations of the Hellenistic 'Middle Stoa'. These were the old Athenian heroes who gave their names to the ten official divisions of the Athenian citizenry.

As THE AGORA provided the setting for many scenes in Socrates' life, so also it witnessed the judicial proceedings leading to his death. We have already seen that his conversation with Euthyphro took place while he was waiting in the Stoa Basileios to appear before the King Archon on a charge of impiety. The usual procedure in most cases, both public and private, was that the prosecutor, who might be any Athenian citizen, came to the defendant with one or two witnesses, stated his plaint and summoned him to appear before the appropriate magistrate on a particular day. In this case Meletus probably had no difficulty finding Socrates either in the Agora or in a palaestra near by, and when the appointed day came Socrates broke off the current conversation (the one with Theaetetus according to Plato) and went to the Stoa Basileios. There Meletus made his formal accusation of impiety in the presence of the King Archon, who had it written on a whitened board and posted on Athens' public noticeboard in front of the statues of the Eponymous Heroes. More than seven centuries later the sophist Libanius wrote a Defence of Socrates in which he asked why Socrates had not been charged long before if he had really been doing wrong (*Apologia Socratis* 43): 'Have we not had a plethora of notices posted by the Eponymous Heroes. . . ? But never a one saying that so-and-so son of such-and-such indicted Socrates of Alopeke.'

In trials such as that of Socrates there was a presiding magistrate but no judge and no lawyers but only the plaintiff and defendant. The jury of 500 listened to speeches on both sides and voted first on the indictment, whether the plaintiff had made his case or whether the defendant was not guilty as charged. If the defendant was convicted a second pair of speeches followed in which each side proposed a penalty, and the jury voted a second time between the proposals. In this case we do not know how the prosecution may have spoken except from hints in the speeches of defence put in Socrates' mouth by two contemporaries, Plato and Xenophon. It seems likely that both Meletus and Anytus spoke, the former emphasizing Socrates' failure to recognize the city's gods and his dangerous influence on the young, the latter urging that either Socrates should never have been brought to trial or, since he had been, he must not escape death, 'saying to you that if I escaped "Your sons, who are already practicing what Socrates teaches, will all be utterly corrupted" ' (Plato, *Apology* 29b).

That Socrates himself said many of the things reported by Plato and Xenophon is likely because they were writing for an audience that included many who were present at the trial either as jury or spectators. And what Xenophon wrote that he heard from Hermogenes both has a ring of truth and lends credence to the informal nature of the *Apologies*:

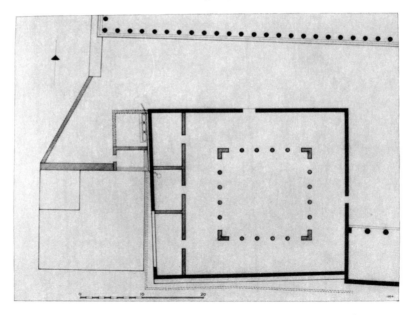

22. Plan of the Heliaia in the 2nd century B.C. This most important of Athenian courts may have been the site of Socrates' trial. See Figure 2 for location. The earlier form of the building, which dates from the 6th century B.C., is less certain.

Hermogenes: After Meletus had indicted him I heard him talking about everything else except the case and so I said to him that he ought to consider how he would defend himself. At first he said, 'Do I not seem to you to have been practicing for this throughout my life?'

And surely there is nothing prophetic about Callicles' censure of Socrates in Plato's *Gorgias* (486) for devoting himself to philosophical inquiry instead of acquiring wealth and renown: 'For if someone should hale you off to prison saying that you did wrong when you had not, you know that you would not be able to cope, but you would become dizzy and stand gaping without a word to say, and coming into court, even if you had a poor and feeble accuser, you would die if he wished to propose death as a penalty.' As a matter of fact it was probably Socrates' use of his usual dialectic that provoked the jurors and made them vote against him. In the *Theaetetus* of Plato (172) Socrates seems to say that it is the privilege and mark of a philosopher and free man to be condemned since only one who has learned to flatter and deceive like a slave can win in the courts.

23. Judicial paraphernalia: wheel-shaped ballots with solid and hollow hubs for acquittal or condemnation; models of the Agora water clock (*clepsydra*) show how it was used for timing speeches of prosecution and defence.

24. View (from north) of remains identified as those of the State Prison in which Socrates spent his last days.

WHEN THE JURORS voted 280 to 220 to convict Socrates, the prosecution proposed death as the penalty. Socrates did not then propose exile, which the jurors might have preferred as getting rid of him without the onus of execution, but he provoked them still further by what must have appeared the frivolous suggestion that he be given free meals at state expense as a public benefactor. Plato has him go on (*Apology* 38b) to propose more seriously a fine which his friends will help pay, but Xenophon (*Apology* 23) insists that he refused either to propose a penalty or to let his friends do so on the grounds that this would be to admit that he had done wrong. In either case the jurors seem to have resented his attitude as arrogant and voted by an even larger majority the penalty of death.

At the conclusion of the trial Socrates was taken to the prison, there to stay until the execution could be carried out. This was delayed because it was a time of festival during which ritual purity required that no public execution take place. His friends were allowed to visit him, and as a result Plato's reports of prison conversations in the *Crito* and *Phaedo* include information about what it was like 'inside' and provide some local color.

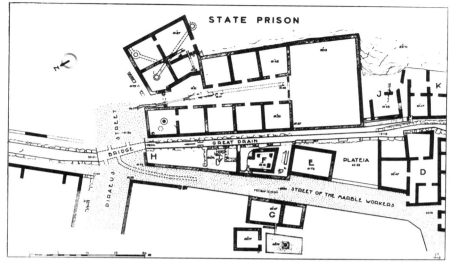

25. Ground plan of the prison: the main gate at left leads into a corridor off which the cells open and which ends in a large courtyard; the foundations of the semi-detached wing at upper left suggest that it was two-storied. The 'suite' at lower left boasts an inner room with bathing facilities.

Crito was such a regular visitor and had sufficiently tipped the guard that he was let in even before sunrise. Coming as he did with news of the festival's approaching end, he was more urgent than ever that Socrates allow a prison escape to be planned so that he might live in exile. That the prison was structurally secure is suggested by the contemplated means of rescue, that is, payment both to men who would get Socrates out and to potential informers to muzzle them.

The picture in the *Phaedo* is of Socrates' friends gathered together with him in the prison on the last day of his life. The group was rather large; fourteen are mentioned by name and 'some others' passed over anonymously may have brought the total up to eighteen. Phaedo tells his eager audience in Phlius how on that day as on previous days the friends had gathered at dawn in the court near by to wait till the prison was opened. If this literary scene-setting is grounded, as it were, in the buildings of the Agora, the court in which they met was probably the Heliaia, a little over a hundred meters to the northeast of the prison. The size of the individual rooms or cells in the prison is such that a good number of people could be comfortably accommodated: they are 4.50 m. square, and if wooden benches were set along three of the walls some twenty-six people would each have 45 cm. sitting space, leaving the parts of the fourth wall on either side of the door for the cot and other furniture of the cell's regular occupant.

When Phaedo and the others entered the room they found Socrates' wife and youngest child with him. His leg iron had just been removed, and after sending Xanthippe and the boy away he sat on his bed rubbing his leg and musing about the relation of pleasure and pain. The conversation then turned to his attitude toward death and proofs of the soul's immortality, an appropriate swan song (to which Socrates himself likened it) for a philosopher who accepted death as perhaps the greatest of goods. In one of the interludes Phaedo describes how he was sitting on a low stool by Socrates' bed, so that Socrates was able to stroke his hair and so that we may increase the cell's potential seating capacity to twenty-seven!

In answering objections to his proofs Socrates shows how his present beliefs and understanding came only after he had abandoned his youthful forays into natural science and the various 'pre-Socratic' accounts of cause and effect in the real world. It is not only a good literary device (for Plato) and a good rhetorical ploy (for Socrates) to ground the present argument firmly and show from what it sprang, but it is also a demonstration of the commonly

26. The State Prison in restored drawing which shows the northeast wing as guard tower, with offices perhaps below.

held belief that a dying man's whole life seems to unroll before his eyes. Then Socrates' final proof of the soul's immortality involves an exposition of the so-called Theory of Ideas which demonstrates the existence of unchanging and eternal forms or concepts separate both from the material world and from human thoughts about it. Having thus shown the world he was leaving to be but an inconstant shadow, Socrates was ready to take his departure into the light of eternity.

He went to an inner room to bathe, to spare those who would lay out his body that chore. This report makes it possible to determine which of the prison cells Socrates occupied, for only one has access to an inner room, the second on the right of the corridor. That the first room on the right not only has no access from the corridor but also has facilities for bathing surely confirms the identification. When he had bathed, his three sons and the women of his household were taken to him in the inner room where he spoke with them and Crito. Then having sent them on their way he returned to where his friends had remained, spending the interval in mutual expressions of regret at their coming bereavement. It was then near sunset, but he sat down and continued to converse until presently the servant of the Eleven (police

27. View (during excavation) of the inner room with basin and large jar set into the floor. The basin is about a third of a meter in both diameter and depth; the jar almost one and a half meters.

28. Thimble-sized terracotta vessels used for drugs and medicine. The thirteen found in the Annex could have been used for the executioner's hemlock which was put up in the exact amounts necessary for an effective dose.

magistrates) came to ask Socrates' forgiveness and to announce that the time to administer the fatal potion had come. Despite the urging of some of his friends to delay and enjoy one last dinner with them he sent the man off to prepare the hemlock. Since no trace of kitchen facilities has been found in the prison, it is assumed that the simple meals of regular residents were prepared on a small brazier somewhere in the Annex, but food and drink for a large farewell party would have to be sent in from elsewhere.

Following the directions given to him, Socrates drank the poison and then walked around until his legs grew heavy. Then he lay down on his bed, re-proaching his friends for weeping: 'It was mostly for this that I sent the women away, so that there might not be this kind of disturbance; for I have heard that one ought to die in peace.' Soon the attendant pinched his leg and asked if he felt anything; Socrates said no. Gradually the numbness spread upwards. When it reached his abdomen, he covered his face and said to Crito: 'I owe a cock to Asclepius; do not forget, but pay it.' These were his last words, and 'this was the end of our comrade, a man who was best, wisest and most just of all we had known' (*Phaedo* 117d–118).

29. At left, fragment of a small marble statuette found in one of the rooms of the Prison Annex with pottery from the Hellenistic period. Compare the complete British Museum statuette of Socrates (right). Perhaps the prison piece was a memento of a famous early resident who had been more elaborately memorialized with a life-size bronze statue by Lysippus, of which this might be a copy.

THAT THE ATHENIANS soon regretted their execution of Socrates is shown by the commission to a famous sculptor for a statue of him to be set up in the Pompeion where the Panathenaic procession had its origin. This belated recognition may have resulted from Athenian dismay at the outsiders' reaction which Socrates predicted (Plato, *Apology* 38c): 'For the sake of very little time, gentlemen, you will have to hear from those who wish to criticize Athens that you killed Socrates, a wise man. For they will say that I was wise even if I am not, wishing to reproach you.'

That the Agora was all things to all men Socrates is living proof. As a gathering place it was where he could go to open men's minds and act the gadfly on the body politic, but as the center of the politics, commerce and litigation from which true philosophers stand aloof it was the symbol of all he wished to abjure. So it was right and fitting that as he spent much of his life in the Agora as gathering place so it was the Agora as nurse of demagogues and bigots that saw his death.

LIST OF ILLUSTRATIONS

Front Cover. Bone figure of Socrates, Agora BI 21
Title page. Hemlock, courtesy of Dr. John Tucker
Back Cover. Seal of the American School of Classical Studies at Athens